DOCUMENTING EMPLOYABILITY & EARNING CAPACITY IN MATRIMONIAL CASES

BY

EDMOND PROVDER

CERTIFIED REHABILITATION COUNSELOR

DIPLOMATE, AMERICAN BOARD OF VOCATIONAL EXPERTS

Jacobs & Whitehall
21750 Hardy Oak Blvd
Suite 104 – 51700
San Antonio, Texas 78258
www.jacobsandwhitehall.com
(888) 570-7338

Ordering Information:

Quantity sales. Special discounts are available on quantity purchases by corporations, associations, and others. For details, contact the publisher at the address above.

Orders by U.S. trade bookstores and wholesalers. Please contact Jacobs & Whitehall: Tel: (888) 991-2766 or visit www.jacobsandwhitehall.com.

Printed in the United States of America

Published in 2022

ISBN: 978-1-954506-43-5

FOREWORD

Due to the Pandemic and resultant Recession/Depression the use of Vocational Experts has substantially increased. Many Matrimonial attorneys do not comprehend how the use of Vocational Experts can assist them in resolving their cases. Therefore, I have written this step by step book to assist attorneys and their clients to understand how Vocational Experts can help them in their matrimonial cases. I have incorporated many case examples to illustrate the type of cases a Vocational Expert can be useful.

Dedication

Without the assistance of the staff at Occupational Assessment Services I would never have been able to write this book. So I thank each employee, Erika, Carla, Katrina, Abi, Janeen, Roger, and Laura. In addition, the support of my children Veronica and Daniel have helped me in moving forward with this book. Lastly, I want to thank all the matrimonial attorneys who I have worked with over my many years and provided me with the various cases that serve as an illustration and foundation for this book.

ACKNOWLEDGEMENTS

In the 1990's I was working as a vocational expert for more than 15 years when I was approached by Cary Cheifetz now a Partner at Ceconi & Cheifetz in New Jersey contacted me about a Matrimonial Case. After the case concluded, Mr. Cheifetz and I wrote the two definitive articles on Using Vocational Expert in Divorce Cases. To date there has been only several articles and one book on this subject.

DISCLAIMER

This publication is intended to be used for educational purposes only. No legal advice is being given, and no attorney-client relationship is intended to be created by reading this material. The author assumes no liability for any errors or omissions or for how this book or its contents are used or interpreted or for any consequences resulting directly or indirectly from the use of this book. For legal or any other advice, please consult an experienced attorney or the appropriate expert who is aware of the specific facts of your case and is knowledgeable of the law in your jurisdiction.

Occupational Assessment Services, Inc.
www.oasinc.org
(800) 292-1919

Table of Contents

INTRODUCTION

As Bob Dylan says in his famous song, "The times they are a-changin."

According to the National Bureau of Economic Statistics, we have been in a recession since 2020 due to the COVID-19 pandemic. The changing economic times have, and will continue to have, a great impact on vocational experts as they evaluate the employability of spouses in divorce cases.

Since publishing my landmark articles, "The Use of Vocational Experts in Matrimonial Cases" and "Evaluating the Disabled Spouse," in the early 1990s, the courts have experienced increased use of vocational experts in matrimonial cases. Since then, the only other article published on the topic has been by Brett Kimmel and Rona Wexler, "Vocational Experts Help Decide Parties Ability to Work," in the New York Law Journal (2/10/08) and one book entitled "Work and Divorce" by Betty Kohlenberg (2013).

Nothing has been written for the attorney looking for guidance in this important new area of vocational expert testimony, especially in the current recession. Spousal circumstances change in a bad economy, in ways we could not foresee.

For that reason, I was asked to set forth some of my own experiences and thoughts on this subject. I hope this book will provide a brief navigational guide to use when a vocational expert is required to answer questions as to a spouse's employability and earning capacity, as well as what to expect from vocational experts and how their use can ultimately benefit your client's case.

CHAPTER I:

THE PANDEMIC EFFECT

The most recent research from the New York State Department of Labor reports New York City's seasonally adjusted unemployment rate was 7.6 percent in January 2022 and 5.2% in New Jersey. The number of unemployed in New York State is 501,000 at present.

According to a survey from LegalTemplates, COVID-19 increased tensions in marriages and negatively impacted many relationships. The company reports a 34% increase in divorce agreements compared to the same period in 2019. Pandemic-related stressors played a big part in this. Concerns over quarantine conditions, unemployment, financial strain, death of loved ones, illness, childcare, remote schooling, and mental illness spilled over into marriages and relationships.

Due to working from home and limited travel, families spent more continuous time together than ever before, oftentimes without being well-prepared to do so. For couples with relationships that were already struggling, this likely increased tension and, in some cases, brought couples to the realization they could be happier apart than together.

It has never been so important for matrimonial attorneys to understand the need to document the employability and earning capacity of a spouse. According to the most recent U.S. Department of Labor Statistics (September 2021), the United States has 7.67 million unemployed persons. We are in a severe recession due to the pandemic, resulting in 2.59 million jobs lost. The economic climate will make it harder for a spouse to obtain employment if unemployed. It will take them longer to obtain employment, and the employment they obtain may pay less than their prior job.

The divorce attorney requires a vocational expert to assist in documenting the economic impact of the recession due to the pandemic on their client and/or spouse.

One of the other factors resulting in the increased use of vocational experts in matrimonial cases is the new alimony tax rule. This regulation has changed the way alimony is taxed. Under old federal tax laws, alimony payments were 100% tax-deductible by the payor and 100% taxable for the recipient. The new rules reverse this. The tax burden for alimony falls squarely on the shoulders of the paying spouse, who must now claim this money as part of taxable income. As tax liability shifts back to the higher earner, and income is generally taxed at a higher rate, less money is available for parties to divide between them and share with their children.

Within the new tax landscape, it is a given that a typical payor strategy will be figuring out how to minimize alimony at all costs. This is where a vocational expert can be used to determine and impute earnings to the spouse, thus reducing the amount of alimony paid.

Vocational experts are professionals who have training and experience working with people who have sustained "life-altering events." The Association of Rehabilitation Economic Association defines a vocational expert as "an expert in the areas of vocational rehabilitation, vocational and earning capacity, [and] lost earnings...They perform evaluations for purposes of civil litigation."

(www.a-r-e-a.org). Another general definition states that "A vocational expert is an authority in the areas of vocational rehabilitation, vocational and earning capacity. They perform evaluations for purposes of civil litigation, as an aspect of economic damages."

The vocational expert assists individuals in locating employment and adjusting to their limitations. In terms of matrimonial and spousal support cases, a spouse who has been a homemaker and has not worked for an extended period of time is considered to have a disability and, thus, can benefit from the services of a vocational expert.

With the advent of increased matrimonial litigation, attorneys realize the need to document the employability and earning capacity of a spouse. Due to their experience, vocational experts have been utilized by matrimonial lawyers to bridge the gap between a stay-at-home spouse and his/her potential employability. As a result of the pandemic and ensuing recession, vocational experts have been increasingly asked to evaluate cases involving change of circumstances, child maintenance orders, and unemployed or underemployed spouses, as well as to determine the earning capacity of homemakers re-entering the labor market.

In order to evaluate a spouse's employability and earning capacity, the attorney should retain a rehabilitation counselor or vocational expert who is knowledgeable regarding the types of jobs a person out of the workforce can perform, the local labor market, and wage statistics. The use of an employability expert can assist in resolving the divorce case pre-trial.

Vocational experts were first used in Social Security Disability cases stemming from Kerner v. Flemming, 283 F.2d 916 (2d Cir. 1960). In this case, vocational experts are defined as professionals who are educated, trained, and skilled in job placement; knowledgeable about labor market conditions; and can formulate vocational opinions of an individual based on their age, education, background, work experience, and medical condition(s).

The opinions presented by vocational experts should be based on their education, training, experience, and the information contained in various traditional vocational sources, including private, federal, and state government publications. The current knowledge and methods used in forensic vocational rehabilitation are applied in determining the spouse's employability and earning capacity.

The U.S. Bureau of Labor Statistics is revamping job categories using the new Occupational Requirement

Survey (ORS). In its third of five years of research, the ORS provides greater detail as to the physical, manipulation, positional, mental, and environmental training required of jobs in the national economy. With the ORS, the government is moving away from the traditional resource, Department of Labor's Dictionary of Occupational Titles (DOT) (1991), to this updated resource which includes fewer occupations.

In addition, vocational opinions should be based on the information available at the time of the evaluation. This information includes medical and other records, the individual's history (as obtained from the standardized vocational interview), vocational testing results (if applicable), professional clinical judgment, and labor market research.

QUALIFICATIONS

A vocational expert is no different from any other expert you will retain in your case in that you want to retain one who understands matrimonial litigation.

An employability expert should have at least a master's degree in rehabilitation counseling from an accredited university—the professional degree in the field. National certification as a rehabilitation counselor is a minimal credential, as many states do not have state licensing.

Certified rehabilitation counselors have been accredited by the Commission on Rehabilitation Counselor Certification (crccertification.com). The certification requirements consist of completing a master's degree in rehabilitation counseling, supervision by a certified rehabilitation counselor, and successfully passing an examination.

A second desirable certification for a rehabilitation expert is approval by the American Board of Vocational Experts (abve.net). This organization was formed in the mid-1980s and is comprised of rehabilitation professionals working in the forensic area. There are less than 475 rehabilitation experts in the country approved by the Board. Due to their interest in forensic rehabilitation, these experts are probably the most knowledgeable in evaluating impaired work capacity.

In the private sector, the International Association of Rehabilitation Professionals (rehabpro.org) has a division for professionals interested in forensic rehabilitation issues. Membership is important as the yearly conferences contain the most up-to-date information.

A very desirable factor in retaining an employability expert is past testimony experience. If the expert has worked for the Office of Disability Adjudication and Review (Social Security Administration), he or she will have been cross-examined numerous times regarding employability. In addition, the cachet of being a witness for the federal government makes the vocational expert qualified at trial.

The individual must be a practitioner and have actual hands-on experience locating jobs for disabled and non-disabled people. Your expert should also have experience working in matrimonial cases. Since this is a relatively new area, you will be relying on the expert for guidance. The expert should be available to guide you as to the information and processes required to perform the evaluation

Knowledge

The vocational expert should be knowledgeable and aware of the local and national job market, as well as the salaries for particular occupations in your region. This is especially important in rural areas, where employment opportunities and salary levels are limited. Certainly, you should avoid individuals with no practical experience, as theory and reality in placing the persons in jobs are two different concepts.

If evaluating a disabled spouse, the expert should be a rehabilitation counselor. A rehabilitation counselor will be knowledgeable in the limitations resulting from the impairment, and can assist the attorney in quantifying this information through a medical exam. Assessing a disabled spouse's employability requires an employability expert knowledgeable in the requirements for competitive job placement of persons with a medical condition.

One of the major dilemmas facing the attorney in selecting an expert is whether to use a virgin witness or an experienced one. Having performed expert testimony work as part of my rehabilitation practice since 1977, it is my opinion that the attorney should avoid the inexperienced vocational witness, as it will only cost time and money and may adversely affect your case. An experienced vocational expert witness will probably have evaluated matrimonial cases similar to yours and will know how to handle your case cost-effectively and efficiently—providing you with the documentation you require in a form useful in your divorce case.

When the case goes to court, the employability expert will be able to consult with you in advance to guide you through the process of direct and cross-examination. The experienced vocational expert will know how to communicate and educate the judge as to the results of the vocational evaluation, as well as to the employability opinions and the basis for such opinions. In a recent case, a spouse was evaluated by a so-called vocational expert who was state certified as a marriage and family counselor. The report created by this counselor was so poor he was not produced as a witness at trial.

I recently participated in a matrimonial case in which the judge made several rulings from the bench, which changed the parameters underlying my initial opinions as to the employability of the spouse. The judge asked many probing questions regarding the spouse's employability and the amount of time required of the spouse to obtain employment. Only an experienced witness can be aware of the interactions in court proceedings and be flexible and prepared enough to respond to any changes.

SELECTION

The selection of the expert reflects on the attorney's competence in their client's mind, as well in the eyes of the opposing attorney and judge.

The employability expert should be objective

and perform a comprehensive evaluation. Consider how the individual will relate to the evaluee. He or she should not overreach but should develop an opinion that details the employability and earning capacity based on the realistic circumstances of the case.

In selecting an expert, contemplate if he or she has experience in matrimonial cases similar to the one at hand. Many vocational experts have never done family law cases nor worked with disabled persons. Retaining an expert with experience in similar cases will save an attorney time and money as he or she will not be paying for the expert to learn on the job.

Another area to pay close attention to is the forensic orientation of the expert. Does he or she perform work mainly for husbands or wives? For instance, some vocational experts specialize in only evaluations of the wife. If an expert's work is dramatically skewed toward one group or the other, his or her assessment of the spouse's employability and earning capacity may not be objective. In a recent case, the opposing expert testified that a well-known politician and highly educated husband was "toxic" due to adverse publicity and therefore unemployable. The judge in the case totally disregarded the expert's conclusions, finding his testimony "tainted" since he only evaluated husbands for wives.

The attorney should not be afraid to bring in an out-of-town expert, especially now that many court venues allow virtual testimony. You want to retain the most experienced vocational expert you can locate. Time and time again, I have seen opposing counsel retain a local expert with minimal experience in employability who cannot stand up to cross-examination. This is especially detrimental when an experienced expert coaches the opposing attorney. Often, the result has been a favorable decision for the attorney who hired the most qualified expert.

Locating Employability Experts

There are only about 120,200 rehabilitation counselors in the United States. Many are employed by state rehabilitation agencies, thus being discouraged from performing work in the forensic area.

The Social Security Administration has individual contracts with 1,150 rehabilitation professionals to serve as vocational experts to testify in Social Security Disability proceedings. Less than one-third of these individuals have been able to take their knowledge and move on to perform forensic evaluations. Even fewer do matrimonial cases.

However, there are usually at least several rehabilitation experts in a particular geographic area capable of performing forensic evaluations. One of the best ways to locate a vocational expert is to ask a colleague who has a matrimonial practice. The attorney can also contact a local university that offers a rehabilitation counseling program and ask one of the professors for a referral.

Local legal publications, such as the New Jersey Law Journal, New York Law Journal, and Massachusetts Lawyers Weekly, provide listings of various types of experts in their "Experts Services" section, as does

Trial Magazine.

Several directories are published listing vocational experts: Seak Expert Witness Directory (www.seakexperts.com), Thomson Reuters eBook Edition Lawyer's Desk Reference, JurisPro Expert Witness Directory (www.jurispro.com), and ALM Witness Directory (www.almexperts.com).

An attorney can also use a forensic expert service, such as the Expert Institute, IMS Expert Services, or the Technical Advisory Services for Attorneys (TASA), a national organization based in Blue Bell, Pennsylvania.

CHAPTER II:

WHEN IS AN EMPLOYABILITY EVALUATION REQUIRED?

As discussed in Chapter 1, due to the pandemic and its effects, vocational experts have been increasingly asked to evaluate cases involving change of circumstances, review of child maintenance orders, unemployed or underemployed spouses, and the earning capacity of homemakers (re-)entering the labor market. An attorney can use a vocational expert in several different ways to prove the employability and earning capacity of a spouse.

The most common type of case involves a wife who has been a homemaker, usually in her mid-40s to early 50s, who has spent the past 20 years taking care of the home and raising the couple's children. She has not worked during these child-raising years. She has managed the home, handled the family's financial matters, and cared for the children. The wife claims she is not employable and has no earning capacity, even though she has a college degree. She seeks alimony from the husband.

An employability evaluation is needed if the request for alimony and support is substantial. The fact that a person is not working, and has been out of the labor market, does not necessarily indicate they are unemployable with no earning capacity. The main questions in matrimonial cases are: What skills and aptitudes does this spouse possess so that he or she can be employed in the local labor market? What could he or she earn by doing so? A vocational expert will assess the spouse and reach a vocational opinion that may resolve the case.

Additional questions to consider may be: What is the cost of providing the spouse with further education or technical training to increase his or her chances of employability? What can he or she expect to earn after receiving this training? A vocational expert can testify on these facts, given their experience in recommending services for clients and placing individuals into jobs.

The second most common circumstance for using a vocational expert is with an underemployed spouse. It is not uncommon that a spouse will change or lose a job prior to or during divorce. Similarly, a professionally employed spouse, such as a physician, therapist, or consultant, can regulate and reduce the number of hours they work. The spouse reduces their hours to artificially demonstrate a significant reduction in earnings.

A vocational assessment is necessary to demonstrate the spouse's actual employability and earning capacity in these cases. Questions as to this spouse's employability and earning capacity can be answered by a vocational expert. He or she will perform a transferability-of-skills analysis, based on past education and employment, as well as a local labor market survey, researching job openings and salaries of these occupations.

The final occurrence in which the need for an expert is required is with a disabled spouse or child. It is not uncommon for a spouse to allege a physical or emotional disability, making them unemployable. In such a case, it is important to retain a vocational expert who is also a rehabilitation counselor with experience working with disabled people. This expert will assist in obtaining information regarding the spouse's physical and/or emotional limitations, if any, and determine what employment opportunities are available to them.

For a severely disabled spouse, who has a lifetime care need, they must demonstrate the cost of their medical needs due to his or her severe medical condition. In this situation, the vocational expert constructs a life care plan that researches and details the spouse's needs, and the costs of the required services to meet these needs in their geographical area. In the case of a couple with a severely disabled child, a life care plan will be used to demonstrate the amount of child support required.

CHAPTER III:

THE EMPLOYABILITY EVALUATION – METHODOLOGY

Once retained by the attorney, a vocational expert will schedule an appointment to perform a vocational evaluation of the spouse. The vocational expert will request that you forward the pertinent case documents prior to the evaluation.

Prior to performing an evaluation, a vocational information form is forwarded to the attorney to be completed by each spouse.

In addition, a request is made for a copy of the spouse's deposition transcript, if one is available. If the spouse is making an allegation of a disability affecting his or her employability, the vocational expert should be provided with copies of all pertinent medical reports and hospital records (usually, only discharge summaries are needed). Since the vocational expert cannot interpret medical reports, a residual functional capacity evaluation form may be sent to the attorney to be filled out by their expert physician. This quantifies the client's physical and/or mental condition in a manner that the vocational expert can use.

At the time of the appointment, the vocational expert will conduct a vocational evaluation of the spouse. It is requested that the spouse's attorney not be present during the evaluation. If the attorney is present, he or she may not interfere with the evaluation nor influence what the spouse says. In a recent contentious case, the vocational evaluation was performed via a recorded Zoom video conference with a court reporter taking down the evaluation.

The evaluation is a four-part procedure. The initial part of the evaluation consists of a document review, followed by a standard vocational interview of the spouse to obtain information regarding his or her background, education, work history, and medical condition(s). Observations made during this interview are an important part of the assessment, which is why a Zoom [or in-person] conference is used for the evaluation. The spouse's demeanor and physical appearance are noted.

On occasion, a document review and standard vocational interview may be sufficient to perform an assessment of employability and earning capacity. Based on the record review and the information obtained in the vocational interview, a battery of vocational tests may be administered. The test battery consists of tasks measuring work abilities, aptitudes, and skills in a wide range of occupations found in the labor market.

One of the vocational evaluation purposes is to assess any transferable skills the spouse may have learned through education, training, or past work experience. These skills are measured, and an assessment is made as to what other jobs could be performed utilizing these skills. For example, a spouse with a high school education may have worked as a telemarketer or sales clerk. The spouse may be able to utilize these skills to work as an insurance or real estate salesperson. These positions exist in greater numbers and pay more.

The ability or inability to transfer skills is assessed in the vocational evaluation and impacts the employability and earning capacity of a spouse.

CHAPTER IV:

ASSESSING EMPLOYABILITY AND EARNING CAPACITY

The results of the vocational evaluation enable the expert to render an opinion as to the employability and earning capacity of the spouse. Based on the results, he or she will formulate a list of jobs the spouse can perform. A job survey is performed, involving contact with various local employers to ascertain the availability and salaries of these jobs.

A spouse's earning capacity is documented by

the vocational expert; differing from the spouse's historical past earnings. For example, if the spouse was a homemaker, he or she may have no past earnings. The vocational expert should look at the spouse's earning potential versus their actual past earnings in such cases. In either case, the vocational expert evaluates the jobs the individual can now perform, based on his or her education and past work experience, and assigns a dollar value to these jobs using local labor market information published by the state or federal department of labor.

CHAPTER V:

VOCATIONAL TESTING

Based on the record review and information obtained in the vocational interview, a battery of occupational tests measuring vocational capacity may be administered. The purpose of the testing is to assess the spouse's employability by measuring their aptitudes and skills. If the spouse alleges a physical or mental impairment, the testing becomes an important part of the assessment.

Standardized tests are administered to assess

the spouse's ability to be employed in the local labor market. The testing evaluates the spouse's ability to perform sedentary, light, medium, heavy, and very heavy types of work activities, as they exist in the labor market and are defined in the U.S. Department of Labor's Dictionary of Occupational Titles.

Interest and aptitude testing may sometimes be administered to assess vocational potential and capacity. The test battery consists of tasks that measure functional academic level, abilities, aptitudes, and physical capacity. The vocational evaluation results are compared to the levels of people working in the industry to ascertain the evaluee's ability to be competitively employed.

Several different types of tests may be administered, based on the United States Government's General Aptitude Test Battery (GATB), to measure six aptitudes. When long-distance testing is required, the CareerScope battery may be administered. It can be used to measure the spouse's aptitude in various areas. The CareerScope can also be administered in Spanish with appropriate norms for comparison. The CareerScope test measures the following aptitudes:

- General Learning: The ability to catch on, or understand, instructions and underlying principles. The ability to reason and make judgments.
- Spatial: The ability to comprehend the 2-D representation of 3-D objects. The ability to recognize the relationships resulting from the movement of objects in space.
- Verbal: The ability to understand the meaning of words, sentences, and paragraphs and use them effectively.
- Numerical: The ability to perform arithmetic operations quickly and accurately without using a calculator.
- Form Perception: The ability to perceive pertinent detail in objects or graphic material. The ability to make visual comparisons and see slight differences in shapes, shadings, and lines.
- Clerical Perception: The ability to perceive pertinent detail in written text or tables. Ability to perceive differences in copy, proofread words and

numbers, and avoid computation errors.

- If an in-person evaluation is conducted, emphasis is placed on observing characteristics, such as,
- quality and quantity of the performance,
- ability and tolerance of performing the tasks,
- reaction to changing tasks,
- ability to sustain time pressures inherent to the tasks,
- ability to comprehend oral and written directions,
- physical stamina,
- ability to concentrate, and
- ability to perform at an even and sustained pace.

Each test battery is individually designed based on the spouse's education, training, and past work experience. The evaluation is conducted one-to-one, with the vocational expert observing the spouse's performance throughout testing. The information analyzed consists of the actual test scores and observations regarding the client's behavior while performing the evaluation. The scores are compared to workers in a competitive work situation.

CHAPTER VI:

TRANSFERABILITY OF SKILLS ANALYSIS

Transfer of skills involves the assessment of skills a person used on one job, which can be interchanged or substituted into another job to determine employability. Skills are learned by doing. In the context of Social Security Disability, transferable skills are defined as the assessment of work functions acquired from the performance of semi-skilled, skilled, or professional jobs that can be applied to meet the requirements of other semi-skilled, skilled, or professional jobs.

The U.S. Federal Government states in 20 CFR 404.1568:

(d) Skills that can be used in other work (transferability)—(1)...We consider you to have skills that can be used in other jobs when the skilled or semi-skilled activities you did in the past work can be used to meet the requirements of skilled or semi-skilled work activities of other jobs or kinds of work. This depends largely on the similarity of occupationally significant work activities among different jobs.

(2) How we determine skills that can be transferred to other jobs. Transferability is most probable and meaningful among jobs in which—

(i) The same or lesser degree of skill is required;

(ii) The same or similar tools and machines are used; and

(iii) The same or similar raw materials, products, processes, or services are involved.

Transferable skills can make the difference

between a person working and not working. The Transferability of Skills Analysis (TSA) is the foundation to identify similar or related jobs that are consistent with or equal to the worker's capabilities and functional restrictions. This seven-step process involves identifying jobs in an individual's work history, selecting an occupational code with title, using the DOT or Occupational Information Network (O*Net), profiling the jobs, creating an unadjusted vocational profile, creating the residual functional capacity profile, finding related or similar jobs, and locating open jobs in the local labor market.

Work experience, meaning the skills and abilities acquired by the individual through labor he or she has done, shows the type of employment they may be expected to do. The U.S. Federal Government states in 20 CFR 404.1565:

(a) Work experience means skills and abilities you have acquired through work you have done which show the type of work you may be expected to do. Work you have already been able to do shows the kind of work that you may be expected to do. We consider that your work experience applies when it was done within the last 15 years, lasted long enough for you to learn to do it, and was substantial gainful activity... A gradual change occurs in most jobs so that after 15 years it is no longer realistic to expect that skills and abilities acquired in a job done then continue to apply. The 15-year guide is intended to insure that remote work experience is not currently applied.

The process of establishing work experience is based on a synthesis of information from an individual's history, including medical, psychological, educational, social, and vocational information. Using acquired skills has been proven to be the most cost-effective means of returning an injured worker or one who has been out of the labor market for a while back to gainful employment.

The spouse's past work history and test results, if administered, are analyzed using the Vocational Diagnosis and Assessment of Residual Employability (VDARE) process. The VDARE is an organized and systematic way of assessing transferable work skills and vocational potential. It is a peer-reviewed, published methodology accepted in the field of rehabilitation counseling. The VDARE process uses the spouse's work history as the basis to build an assessment of their vocational functioning. The analysis takes into account the factors of physical demands, working conditions, general educational development, specific vocational preparation, aptitudes, work activities, and work situations. The search is conducted based on Occupational Group Arrangement (OGA), Data People and Things (DPT), Guide for Occupational Exploration (GOE), Work Field (MTEWA), Specific Vocational Preparation (SVP), and DOT Industry.

The OASYS computer program is the best known and most widely used method to conduct a transferability of skills evaluation. It adheres to the operational definition of TSA contained in the U.S. Code of Federal Regulations. OASYS Transferable Skills Analysis captures the skills and abilities learned from past employment and summarizes them in a work history profile. The profile is then modified to reflect the spouse's current abilities. Applying transferable skills analysis rules, the resulting list of occupations by decreasing levels of transferability can be used to match to potential job titles, actual vacancies, and employers likely to hire.

As part of the transferability of skills process, the OASYS computer program is used to obtain a Labor Market Employability Assessment (LMEA) function study, enabling the vocational expert to conduct an employability study to determine the spouse's potential to perform specific jobs within the local labor market. The program allows the vocational expert to create a list of occupations containing selected occupational characteristics, as noted by the U.S. Department of Labor, based on the spouse's education, past and/or current work history, and medical limitations, if any. Almost any combination of descriptors can be used to determine the types of jobs a spouse can perform, given their background.

The OASYS database can assist the vocational

expert in locating occupation information regarding the spouse's past employment and note them in an easy-to-describe format. A transferability of skills assessment will result in a list of O*NET and DOT occupational tasks, performance demands, and descriptors of jobs, as well as U.S., state, and local employment and wage information, as noted by the U.S. Department of Labor.

Research is conducted regarding the level and types of skills, aptitudes, and physical demands required of each job. A transferability of skills analysis is performed to determine the spouse's ability to use their previously learned skills in occupations available within the local labor market.

CHAPTER VII:

WAGE SURVEYS

Once the vocational interview and/or testing results (if required) are analyzed, a determination must be made as to the earnings of occupations the vocational expert believes a spouse can perform.

The employability expert can use four types of wage surveys. The most common surveys used are the Occupational Employment and Wage Statistics (OEWS) surveys conducted by the U.S. Bureau of Labor Statistics (https://www.bls.gov/oes/). As the labor analysts attempt to survey every business in the

United States, these surveys have the greatest number of respondents and, therefore, are the most reliable and valid. The U.S. Bureau of Labor Statistics publishes four different types of surveys.

These wage surveys provide an average of national information (https://www.bls.gov/oes/current/oes_nat.htm), state information (https://www.bls.gov/oes/current/oessrcst.htm), local information using the metropolitan and nonmetropolitan area occupational employment and wage estimates (https://www.bls.gov/oes/current/oessrcma.htm), and wage information by occupational profile (https://www.bls.gov/oes/current/oes_stru.htm).

Each survey has occupational groupings by SOC Code. The surveys cover the number of jobs in each occupational group, the mean and median wages for each, and their average annual salary. Below are samples of the wage surveys for the New York City area in 2020 for sample occupational group

SOC Code	Occupation	Number of Jobs	Mean Hourly Salary	Median Hourly Salary	Mean Average Salary
29-1141	Registered Nurses	173,570	$45.65	$45.63	$94,920
29-1171	Nurse Practitioners	13,760	$61.95	$64.12	$133,380
29-1215	Family Medicine Physicians	3,980	$93.31	$99.74	$207,450
29-2055	Surgical Technologists	5,420	$28.71	$29.29	$60,910
31-1120	Home Health and Personal Care Aides	426,290	$14.89	$15.37	$31,960
33-2011	Firefighters	15,770	$44.02	$40.89	$85,040
41-2031	Retail Salespersons	219,790	$14.80	$17.06	$35,490
41-9022	Real Estate Sales Agents	6,750	$37.38	$47.39	$98,580
53-3032	Heavy and Tractor-Trailer Truck Drivers	64,360	$26.73	$27.38	$56,960
53-3033	Light Truck Drivers	49,200	$19.57	$21.27	$44,230

The 867 wage surveys research Standard Occupational Classification (SOC) is used to research average wage salaries in a particular geographical area. However, the United States Bureau of Labor Statistics wage survey conducted in the New York/Newark area contains only 756 occupational groups so some do not contain information on every SOC codes which may be a limitation on using this research. However, this research is considered as the "Gold Standard" as it is performed by the US Government and researches the greatest amount of local employers.

The second wage survey used by employability experts in divorce cases is generated by the state's Department of Labor. Some of these may be more specific than the U.S. Department of Labor's information. For example, the survey for the state of Texas covers the following cities and areas:

- Alamo
- Borderplex
- Brazos

- Cameron County
- Capitol Area
- Central Texas
- Coastal Bend
- Concho Valley
- Dallas
- Deep East Texas
- East Texas
- Golden Crescent
- Gulf Coast
- Heart of Texas
- Lower Rio Grande
- Middle Rio Grande
- North Central Texas
- Northeast Texas
- North Texas
- Panhandle
- Permian Basin
- Rural Capital Area
- Southeast Texas
- South Plains
- South Texas

- Tarrant County
- Texoma
- West Central Texas

Each survey will provide mean wage information and the number of local jobs for each occupation.

The third type of wage survey is conducted by various websites, such as Payscale.com, Ladders.com, and Salary.com. These are wages obtained via individuals searching for jobs and voluntarily providing their geographical and wage information. There are no validity or reliability studies performed on this information, as there are with government surveys. Economic Research Institute (ERI) also provides detailed salary surveys, but there is no information regarding the reliability of this data or how the information is obtained. Recently, Ziprecruiter.com has been providing average salary wages based on ADP data as ADP is an exclusive provider of employee payroll data for ZipRecruiter.

Another type of wage data used is surveys

conducted for specific occupations. It is not unusual for a professional organization to conduct a wage survey of their members to determine earnings information. For example, Medscape provides wage surveys for physician compensation, as does the American Medical Association (AMA) (https://www.ama-assn.org/about/research/how-physicians-get-paid-see-where-you-fit).

The last survey method experts use to determine the earning capacity of a spouse is to obtain the actual salary amount being offered for jobs in the local labor market by looking at advertised job openings and/or calling employers. This information is extremely important, as it demonstrates what a particular job pays in the spouse's local geographical area.

The employability expert should be aware of the various types of labor market surveys to be used to establish the spouse's earning capacity.

CHAPTER VIII:

LABOR MARKET SURVEYS

Once the vocational expert reaches an opinion as to the types of jobs a spouse can perform, it is necessary to demonstrate that these jobs exist in the geographical area wherein he or she resides. To demonstrate the availability of jobs in the local labor market, at times, it is necessary to locate actual job openings.

Establishing the availability of local job openings can be done by calling potential employers. However, the most widely used method by employability experts is to use various internet job search sites. Some of the most widely used sites include,

- Careerbuilder.com,
- Simplyhired.com,
- Indeed.com,
- Ziprecruiter.com, and
- Monster.com.

These labor market surveys should be performed for each occupation the vocational expert opines the spouse can perform. The standard radius for a job search is 50 miles from the spouse's residence.

Research should be conducted using multiple internet sites with the results saved as part of the file. The salaries published for each job should be recorded for inclusion in the vocational report. The number of available jobs, as well as the advertised salaries, should be noted. I like to place this information in chart form, e.g.:

JOB TITLE	# OF ADVERTISED JOBS	ADVERTISED SALARY
Office Manager	15	$75,820
Administrative Assistant	20	$62,050
Customer Service Representative	25	$45,610
Receptionist/Information Clerk	40	$37,550
Order Clerk	35	$40,420
General Clerk	20	$39,580
Information & Record Clerk	14	$51,130
Credit Authorizer	18	$50,700

The employability expert may not have to conduct a detailed labor market survey if the occupations the spouse can perform are common and a significant number of jobs are noted to exist in the local labor market. However, demonstrating that jobs are open and exist within the spouse's geographical area strengthens the vocational expert's opinion, especially if there is a deposition or court testimony in the case.

CHAPTER IX:

THE USE OF THE VOCATIONAL EXPERT IN DEFENSE CASES

In the majority of matrimonial cases in which I have been retained, a vocational expert was hired by the opposing attorney. This expert can assist the opposing attorney in analyzing your client's vocational evaluation report to establish the employability and earning capacity of the spouse. This information assists the attorney in establishing the economic details of the case and may play a role in settling the case.

At times, access to one spouse may be denied to the vocational expert by the opposing attorney or the court. Thus, it is extremely important that the defense adequately prepare the case with regard to completing the Vocational Information Form, which the vocational expert can use in rendering his employability opinion.

In case preparation, the vocational expert can help the defense in case preparation provide an objective assessment of the opposing spouse's employability and earning capacity. He or she can also assist in the cross-examination of the opposing vocational expert.

In several recent matrimonial cases, I have been appointed as the court's expert, agreed upon by both sides. In another case, I worked with both attorneys to obtain the proper documentation to assess a spouse's medical impairment and the impact on her earning capacity and employability.

CHAPTER X:

Employability Expert In Court Testimony

One of the reasons for having an Employability Evaluation prepared in a matrimonial case is to fully document a spouse's earnings and detail the underlying reasons for the expert's vocational opinions. The opinions should be stated within a reasonable degree of certainty. The vocational opinions should be based on the spouse's education and work history, transferable skills, and any physical or mental limitations. An employability evaluation is an objective method of substantiating the spouse's employability and earning capacity.

At the time of trial, the expert may use demonstrative evidence detailing the spouse's past work experience, earnings, wage survey information, and/or labor market survey results. The attorney should have the items utilized in advance of the trial. The content of each exhibit should be covered and testified to at the trial to illustrate the expert's opinions. While giving testimony, the expert should utilize the exhibits to educate the judge as to the individual's employability and earning capacity.

The attorney should ensure the employability expert is ready for a rigorous cross-examination by the opposing attorney. If the expert is experienced and prepared, he or she should be able to handle any questions regarding his or her vocational opinions.

CHAPTER X:

Case Studies And Illustrations

One of the most important parts of a divorce case is for the attorney to know when he or she needs a vocational expert. Therefore, I will discuss the types of cases in which a vocational expert is needed and provide illustrations for each.

Case Study 1: The Homemaker

The most frequent use of an employability expert is when the spouse, usually a wife, has been unemployed for several years, raising the children and taking care of the home. However, given certain circumstances, an evaluation has been conducted of a stay-at-home husband due to the wife having a professional occupation. A contention is made that the homemaker is not employable and has no earning capacity, as they have not recently worked. At times, the wife has a college degree and seeks a large amount of alimony from the husband. The vocational expert will conduct an interview. Based on the spouse's past education and work history, he or she will formulate a vocational opinion, even though the homemaker has been out of the labor market for a number of years. If the request for alimony and support is substantial, an employability evaluation is necessary.

Ms. Green is a 48-year-old law school graduate. She worked as an attorney prior to her marriage. She was licensed as an attorney in two states but stopped practicing to raise two children. The employability expert researched job openings using Indeed.com, Glassdoor.com, Careerbuilder.com, SimplyHired.com, and the state government websites, ultimately locating 12 open jobs she could perform, paying an average of $110,000 per annum. This case resolved based on the vocational report.

The second illustration is Ms. Burke, a 52-year-old homemaker who had two children over the age of 22. She had a bachelor's degree and had been employed as an office helper and clerk prior to her divorce. In addition, she recently obtained her real estate license. The average salary range of a real estate sales agent in her geographical area, based on 460 jobs, was $47,500 to $53,500 per annum. The vocational expert located 15 open and available jobs she could perform given her background. This case was resolved without going to trial.

A third case illustration is Mr. West, a 40-year-old internationally known sports figure. He had won many awards and served as a sports commentator. He testified that he never earned any money, despite owning two fully paid houses and regularly visiting his girlfriend across the country. The vocational expert interviewed and evaluated Mr. West and made a determination, based on his skills and current circumstances, that he could earn up to $75,000 per annum, based on a labor market and wage survey. The case was resolved prior to the vocational expert's deposition.

Case Study 2: The Underemployed Spouse

The second most common circumstance is a spouse who, just prior to the divorce, becomes unemployed or under-employed. It is not uncommon that, prior to divorce, a spouse will change jobs, lose his or her job, or stop working to artificially demonstrate limited or no earnings. A vocational assessment is necessary to demonstrate the spouse's actual employability and earning capacity in the local labor market.

Mr. Jones, a well-known communications executive, was reportedly laid off from his position, which had paid $1 million per year. He was able to obtain another job at a salary of $200,000 per annum with easily obtainable bonuses, which would equal his past earnings. The vocational expert was able to research the communications industry and locate jobs he could perform. The judge imputed an income of $1 million to the husband based on the vocational expert's opinions and ordered alimony based on this amount. Mr. Jones refused to pay and spent his weekends in jail for one year due to his noncompliance.

The second illustration is Ms. Smith, a 45-year-old woman with a master's degree. She had been working as a signage coordinator (interior designer) but quit her job prior to her divorce filing. The vocational expert performed a comprehensive wage and labor market survey to rebut the opposing vocational expert's findings. The judge imputed earnings of $44,680 per annum based on the husband's vocational expert's findings.

The third illustration is Mr. White, who had been employed as a general operations manager, founder, principal (President), and chief operating officer but left his job at the time of his filing for divorce. An internet labor market survey was conducted using Indeed.com, Careerbuilder.com, Monster.com, and SimplyHired.com, revealing at least 10-15 jobs matching his background with annual salaries of $131,900 to $149,300 (based on 5,910 jobs). The judge imputed this amount as his income.

Case Study 3: The Artificial Reduction of Hours/Earnings Spouse

A common occurrence involves a spouse who is a professional, such as a physician, therapist, or consultant, who can regulate the number of hours they work. The spouse reduces their hours and artificially demonstrates a significant reduction in earnings.

Dr. Case, a 60-year-old plastic surgeon, earned $750,000 per annum. However, his earnings became significantly reduced over the years prior to his divorce due to his reducing the number of patients he was seeing. The vocational expert was able to locate open and available jobs in his geographical area, offering salaries equal to his previous earnings. The vocational expert conducted a labor market survey as to the average earnings of a physician in his specialty, and this was the amount imputed to the physician spouse.

The second illustration is Ms. Miranda, a mental health therapist/psychiatrist. She alleged an inability to obtain clients for her practice. However, she had not explored the option of working for mental health agencies as an employee. The vocational expert researched job openings and salaries for licensed mental health counselors, ranging from $194,266 to $242,512 per annum. The mediator considered the vocational expert's opinions, and the case resolved.

The last illustration is Ms. Sharp, who has a master's degree level education and past work experience of professional work as a consultant. She noted an inability to locate employment. The vocational expert performed a labor market and wage survey and located available jobs in her local area paying from $47,720 to $131,450 per annum on a full-time basis.

Case Study 4: The Disabled Spouse

The disabilities claimed by spouses are similar to those encountered in personal injury cases. The disability could be an impairment to the back, leg, arm, hand, or knee; the severity of which can range from a sprained wrist to a fractured leg, to a torn meniscus, to a herniated disc. In addition, conditions such as blindness, deafness, multiple sclerosis, and cancer could also be claimed. In addition, it is not unusual for a spouse to claim an emotional or psychological impairment. The disability could result in the spouse having no loss to a total loss of earning capacity.

At times, a spouse with a medical condition may allege an inability to work due to their being disabled. When the attorney encounters a disabled spouse, it is imperative to retain a vocational expert who is also a rehabilitation counselor as they have experience placing disabled people in jobs. The rehabilitation expert will assist in obtaining medical information regarding the spouse's physical and/or emotional limitations through the use of residual functional capacity evaluation forms to assist in formulating an opinion as to what employment opportunities are available for the disabled spouse.

Ms. Carr, a 52-year-old attorney, was diagnosed with an orthopedic impairment. Due to the residuals of her condition, she was working remotely and reported a substantial reduction in earning capacity. The rehabilitation counselor/vocational expert conducted a standard vocational evaluation interview. He formulated an opinion that she had the capability to perform work as an attorney, which requires sedentary physical demands. The expert noted that she could earn the average salary of attorneys in her state of $175,000 per annum and that her medical condition did not affect her earning capacity.

A second case was Mr. Garden, an executive in the construction industry. He alleged difficulty breathing but exercised daily for up to three hours. Mr. Garden also noted having an emotional condition and was being treated by a therapist. He had not conducted a job search to locate alternative employment. An extensive job search was conducted, and over 40 jobs openings were found ranging from unskilled to skilled work. During deposition testimony, the rehabilitation counselor/vocational expert was able to provide an opinion regarding the husband's earnings capability, ranging from $40,000 to $100,000 per annum.

Depending on the severity of a spouse's disability, he or she may qualify for retraining services sponsored by the state's vocational rehabilitation agency. The provision of these services is usually provided at no cost. As part of the vocational evaluation, the vocational expert considers the spouse's functional limitations, aptitudes, and capabilities as they relate to retraining for other occupations. The expert details possible vocational opportunities, expected salaries after education or training has been received, and the length of time required for training.

Ms. Stone, a 44-year-old communications specialist with two master's degrees, sustained a traumatic sensory nerve hearing loss, causing her employer to place her on long-term disability, paying her 60% of her salary. In addition, she was receiving Social Security Disability benefits, making up 40% of her salary.

The disabled spouse filed a claim for support from her husband in the amount of the potential increase in wages she might have received had she continued to work. The results of the vocational evaluation indicated that, despite her hearing loss, there were technological devices that would enable her to return to her past work or assist her in retraining in desktop publishing. Since she was a Social Security Disability recipient, the state vocational rehabilitation agency would fully pay for any retraining, even if she wanted to go to law school. Lastly, a labor market survey located several employers who were interested in hiring her on a part-time basis, the earnings from which would not affect her other benefits. These earnings would more than make up for any loss of wages she claimed.

Ms. Greene, a 47-year-old woman with one year of college, had her own furniture business until 1999 when she married her husband, who did not want her to work. Due to her divorce, Ms. Greene became severely depressed and sought psychiatric treatment. The psychiatrist noted that her depression negatively affected her memory, concentration, and ability to work on a full-time basis. The performance of vocational testing and a computerized transferability skills analysis indicated she could perform clerical and sales-type jobs. It was determined that due to her psychiatric condition, at best, she could work part-time (20 hours per week) at a rate of $15 per hour until her depression improved. Once her depression had improved, it was the vocational expert's opinion she could work on a full-time basis (40 hours per week) at the same hourly rate.

Case Study 5: The Severely Disabled Spouse or Child

Another circumstance requiring an evaluation is a severely disabled spouse who is unable to care for him or herself. One who requires extensive future medical and home care. This circumstance requires a rehabilitation counselor who is also certified as a life care planner. This expert will

determine the spouse's long-term care needs and objectively demonstrate the cost of medical care required in their geographical area.

When there is a severely disabled child, a life care plan should be used to demonstrate the additional funds required for his or her medical care, thus increasing the amount of child support required.

The initial illustration is Mr. Costa, a 92-year-old man who was wheelchair-bound and required a modified handicap-friendly home environment and extensive home attendant care. Despite having a prenuptial agreement, his spouse questioned the need for these services, and the case proceeded to court. The husband retained a life care planner who detailed his long-term life care plan needs and testified at trial. The wife retained a physician who testified no additional money was required for his care as government insurance would cover these expenses. Despite a court proceeding that extended for months, the judge awarded monthly funds for his care based on the rehabilitation expert life care planner's testimony.

The second case is Kris, a 12-year-old paraplegic male who needed long-term medical care due to his physical impairments. A rehabilitation counselor/life care planner evaluated Kris and developed a life care plan that illustrated his needs, as well as the costs of this care in his local geographical area. The plan was presented to a mediator, and the case resolved with the husband paying the additional amount required for his son's medical treatment and care.

Case Study 6: Spouse Evaluation in a Recession

The current circumstances of the pandemic and recession have affected the availability of work and has affected job salaries. These circumstances require a Vocational Expert to assess the availability and salaries of various jobs in the current labor market.

Mr. Jones, a 52-year-old computer maintenance worker, employed in New York, had been updating software onto mainframe computers for ten years and had not upgraded his computer skills. As his hours began to decrease, due to the recession, his job appeared to be in jeopardy. A headhunter was contacted and confirmed there were limited job openings for a person with his skills. However, he was able to find a consulting company that placed him with a power authority in a western state at a salary of $85,000 per annum versus his prior salary of $130,000.

Mr. Jones now had a steadier job that appeared recession-proof but had to take a $45,000 reduction in salary. The vocational expert evaluated Mr. Jones and confirmed that his obsolete skills provided him with limited job potential. In fact, it was determined that his current wage rate matched the average for jobs available to him in 2020. Mr. Jones applied for a reduction in his child support payments, but the judge dismissed the application stating that he had voluntarily left his initial well-paying job. Apparently, the judge believed it was better for Mr. Jones to be terminated from his prior job than to obtain one that was more secure and recession-proof.

Case Study 7: Reduction Of Child Support Due To Change Of Circumstances

The pandemic and recession have resulted in changes of circumstances for some spouses paying alimony and child support. A Vocational Expert is required to assess the spouse's employability and earning capacity given the changes of circumstances.

A second case involves Mr. Smith, a 48-year-old male who settled his divorce while earning $100,000 per annum with bonuses in the medical industry. Unfortunately, he pleaded guilty to Medicaid fraud which precluded him from working in the medical industry. He filed for a reduction in child support based on his change of circumstances. A labor market snapshot and salary survey were performed, determining he would not pass a background check with his felony conviction. In addition, his conviction came up with a simple internet search. It was determined, at best, Mr. Smith could earn $26,000 per annum performing unskilled jobs such as an assembler, car washer, inspector, and/or deli counter clerk.

Definitions Used By Employability Experts

A good forensic vocational expert will be able to explain to the judge the various important concepts relating to the ability of a spouse to be employed and earn money.

Employability is the standard that is discussed by the vocational expert in relating the evaluee's ability to work. Employability is defined as an estimation of a person's potential for employment in a job within a given local labor market. It assumes the person is feasible for a job based on medical restrictions, physical capacity, education, aptitude, temperament, and geographic location. This is measured by the number of jobs available in a particular labor market.

Often, the concept of employability is confused by attorneys with placeability. Placeability refers to the spouse's potential to be placed in a job within a given labor market. This is the ultimate level of proof, i.e., would a given employer hire this person to perform a job in the local labor market.

Feasibility for competitive employment is assessed by the vocational expert. This is the spouse's acceptability as an employee, in a general sense—as an employer in the competitive labor market has of any employee. This encompasses the spouse's ability to actually perform the demands of a specific job.

Competitive employment is the ability of a person to be employed in the local labor market. Inherent in this concept is the person's capability to get to work on time and work a full eight-hour workday; produce at sufficient speed, endurance, and quality; ability to be consistently acceptable to an employer;

can get along with peers and supervisors.

A vocational handicap is the ability of a person to obtain employment in a particular occupation. Each occupation has specific demands. Some of which are within the spouse's work tolerance and others beyond the work tolerance, thus imposing a vocational handicap. Vocational handicaps involve physical limitations with sitting, standing, walking, lifting, carrying, grasping, and/or manipulating.

Earning capacity is the ability of an individual to earn money in the local or national labor market. This is his or her ability to earn money, not necessarily his or her actual earnings in the local geographical area.

Residual functional capacity is a quantitative measure of an individual's limitations caused by his or her impairment. This encompasses the number of hours in an eight-hour day the individual can sit, stand, walk, lift, and carry. Physicians or vocational experts can render opinions as to the evaluee's capability to perform these activities. A vocational expert takes the person's residual functional capacity into consideration when considering the ability to be employed.

The vocational evaluation of a disabled spouse consists of an assessment of the impact of the functional physical, psychological, and/or cognitive limitations on his or her work capacity. This is performed through a standardized interview with a review of the individual's educational and prior work experience(s), and in some cases, by administering a computerized aptitude test battery. This information is analyzed according to the spouse's ability to work competitively and earn money in the labor market.

The residuals of a person's impairment may affect his or her ability to earn money in the economy. To assess this impact, the vocational expert utilizes information provided in the U.S. Department of Labor's Dictionary of Occupational Titles (DOT), Fourth Edition, Revised 1991. The DOT contains information regarding over 17,500 different occupations found in the local and national labor market.

In this publication, the federal government has formulated a five-point physical demand scale used to classify the exertional requirements of all occupations in the labor market. The definitions of the five physical demand requirements are as follows:

Sedentary Work is defined as "Exerting up to 10 pounds of force occasionally (Occasionally: activity or condition exists up to 1/3 of the time) and/or negligible amount of force frequently (Frequently: activity or condition exists from 1/3 to 2/3 of the time) or constantly (2/3 or more of the time) to lift, carry, push, pull or otherwise move objects, including the human body. Sedentary work involves sitting most of the time but may involve walking or standing for brief periods of time. Jobs are sedentary if walking and standing are required only occasionally (up to 1/3 of the time) and all other sedentary criteria are met."

Light Work is defined as "exerting up to 20 pounds of force occasionally [up to 1/3 of the time], and/or up to 10 pounds of force frequently (1/3 to 2/3 of the time) and/or negligible amount of force constantly (Constantly: activity or condition exists 2/3 or more of the time) to move objects. Physical demand requirements are in excess of those for Sedentary Work. Even though the weight lifted may be only a negligible amount, a job would be rated Light Work; (1) when it requires walking or standing to a significant degree; or (2) when it requires sitting most of the time but requires pushing and/or pulling of arm or leg controls requires exertion; and/or (3) when the job requires working at a production rate pace entailing constant pushing and/or pulling of materials even though the weight of those materials is negligible. NOTE: The constant stress and strain of maintaining a production rate pace, especially in an industrial setting, can be and is physically demanding of a worker even though the amount of force is negligible."

Medium Work is defined as "exerting 20 to 50 pounds of force occasionally [up to 1/3 of the time] and/or 10 to 25 pounds of force frequently [1/3 to 2/3 of the time] and/or greater than negligible up to 10 pounds of force constantly [2/3 or more of the time] to move objects. Physical Demand requirements are in excess of those for Light Work."

Heavy Work is defined as "exerting 50 to 100

pounds of force occasionally [up to 1/3 of the time] and/or 25 to 50 pounds of force frequently [1/3 to 2/3 of the time] and/or 10 to 20 pounds of force constantly [2/3 or more of the time] to move objects. Physical demand requirements are in excess of Medium Work."

Very Heavy Work is defined as exerting in excess of 100 pounds of force occasionally [up to 1/3 of the time] and/or in excess of 50 pounds of force frequently [1/3 to 2/3 of the time] and/or in excess of 20 pounds of force constantly [2/3 or more of the time] to move objects. Physical demand requirements are in excess of Heavy Work."

An understanding of the physical/and or psychological limitations imposed by the evaluee's injury will allow the employability expert to assess the impact of the impairment by placing the person's residual functional capacity into one or more of these physical demand classifications. The rehabilitation expert then considers the spouse's vocational earning capacity given this capacity.

CONCLUSIONS

The use of vocational experts in matrimonial litigation is a relatively new but growing area of expert testimony. Vocational experts can assist the attorney in performing a vocational evaluation to assess a spouse's employability and earning capacity.

The evaluation assesses the spouse's marketable skills and aptitudes, which can be applied in the labor market. The vocational expert documents rehabilitation and retraining opportunities, as well as the costs for these services. Underemployed, unemployed, or disabled spouses can be evaluated to assess their earning capacity.

Local job searches of potential employers for occupations a spouse can perform, linked with local labor market wage information, assist the expert in testifying regarding employability and earning capacity issues. Vocational expert testimony can be useful for either spouse.

Finally, an experienced vocational expert will be able to provide you with the guidance needed to evaluate the employability and earning capacity issues in your divorce case.

ABOUT THE AUTHOR

Edmond Provder is a certified rehabilitation counselor, Diplomate of the American Board of Vocational Experts and certified life care planner who has provided services for the severely disabled since 1973.

Mr. Provder is credentialed by the American Board of Vocational Experts, the Commission on Rehabilitation Counselor Certification and the International Academy of Life Care Planners.

In his extensive, almost 50-year career, Mr. Provder has provided rehabilitation services to, and evaluated the vocational and employability potential of, over nine thousand individuals.

As an expert, Mr. Provder served as a Vocational Expert for the Social Security Administration for nearly a decade by providing impartial vocational testimonies in over 2,500 Social Security Disability Hearings, and he has provided expert witness testimonies in hundreds of cases in federal and state courts throughout the country.

As someone intimately familiar with the needs of disabled individuals, Mr. Provder has developed and administered vocational and rehabilitation programs, including vocational evaluation testing centers and sheltered workshops, for numerous organizations including Mount Sinai Hospital, the South Beach Psychiatric Center, the Staten Island Association for the Visually Handicapped and the Contemporary Guidance Service in New York.

As a recognized authority in his industry, Mr. Provder has been an approved rehabilitation/vocational consultant for the New Jersey Division of Vocational Rehabilitation Services, the New Jersey Commission for the Blind and Visually Impaired and the New York Commission for the Blind and Visually Handicapped. He consulted with the State of New York in developing the program for Vocational Expert testimony in Workers' Compensation cases.

Mr. Provder has been involved in the development of the Phoenix Rehabilitation Center in the Vidigal Favela, Rio de Janeiro Brazil, which is a program to provide rehabilitation services to poor, physically disabled children.

Mr. Provder earned a Bachelor of Science in Rehabilitation Counseling and a Master of Education in Rehabilitation Counseling from Pennsylvania State University. In addition, Mr. Provder has earned 42 credits towards a Doctoral Candidate in Rehabilitation Counseling from New York University, and 128 hours of post-graduate credit in Life Care Planning and Catastrophic Case Management from the University of Florida.

CURRICULUM VITAE

SPECIALTIES

- Vocational, Occupational Assessment, Evaluating Earning Capacity
- Rehabilitation Counseling
- Life Care Planning of the Catastrophically Injured

EDUCATIONAL BACKGROUND

Pennsylvania State University

Bachelor of Science, Rehabilitation Counseling

1971

Pennsylvania State University

Master of Education, Rehabilitation Counseling

1973

POST GRADUATE TRAINING

New York State University

Doctoral Candidate, Rehabilitation Counseling

42 Credits of Completion

1977 - 1987

University of Florida

Intelicus Life Care Planning for Catastrophic Case Management

128 Post Graduate Hours

2003

ACCREDITATIONS

Certified Rehabilitation Counselor

The Commission on Rehabilitation Counselor Certification (License #: 18792)

Certified Life Care Planner

International Academy of Life Care Planners

License #: 18792

Diplomate Certification

The American Board of Vocational Experts

License #: 00448

PROFESSIONAL ASSOCIATIONS

International Association of Rehabilitation Professionals -

Forensic & Life Care Planning Divisions

American Rehabilitation Economic Association

PROFESSIONAL EXPERIENCE

Occupational Assessment Services

Vocational Specialist and Life Care Planner

1981 - Present

Physician Life Care Planning

Vocational Assessment Specialist

December 2011 - November 2016

Social Security Administration

Impartial Vocational Expert Witness in Social Security Disability cases

1977 - 1985; 1997 - 2000

Independent Vocational Consultant

Projects Included: vocational rehabilitation programs for South Beach Psychiatric Center, Staten Island Association for the Visually Handicapped and the Contemporary Guidance Service

1975 - 1979

Supervisor Vocational Facilities, Department of Rehabilitation Medicine - Mount Sinai Hospital

1974 - 1978; 1979 - 1981

Rehabilitation Counselor

Federation of the Handicapped – Higher Horizons for the Homebound

1973 - 1974

Notes

Made in the USA
Las Vegas, NV
10 November 2026

57843567R00059